The Partition of Ireland and the Troubles: The History from the Irish Civil War to the Good Friday

By Charles River Editors

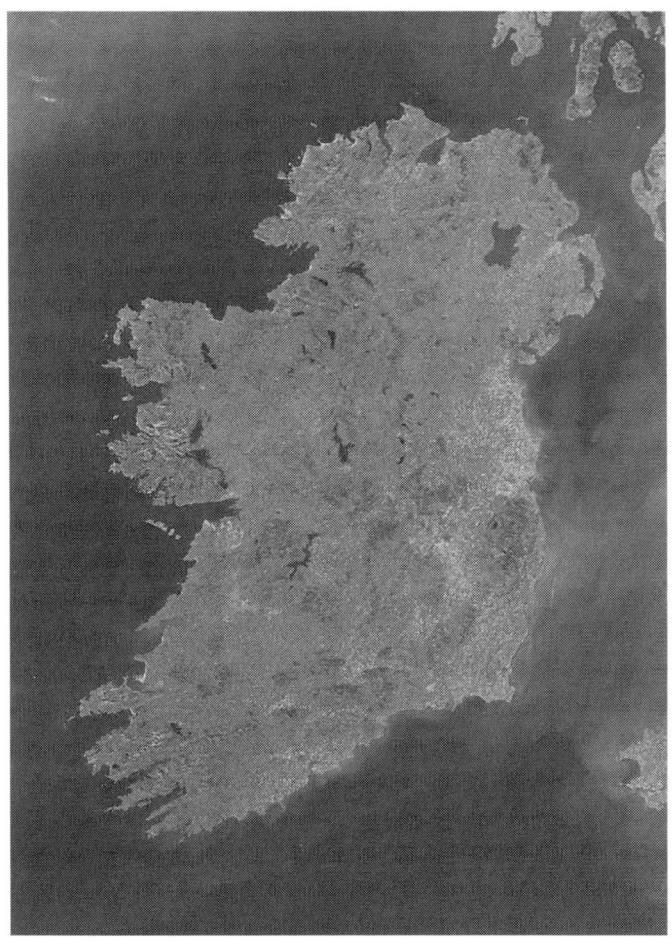

About Charles River Editors

Charles River Editors is a boutique digital publishing company, specializing in bringing history back to life with educational and engaging books on a wide range of topics. Keep up to date with our new and free offerings with this 5 second sign up on our weekly mailing list, and visit Our Kindle Author Page to see other recently published Kindle titles.

We make these books for you and always want to know our readers' opinions, so we encourage you to leave reviews and look forward to publishing new and exciting titles each week.

Introduction

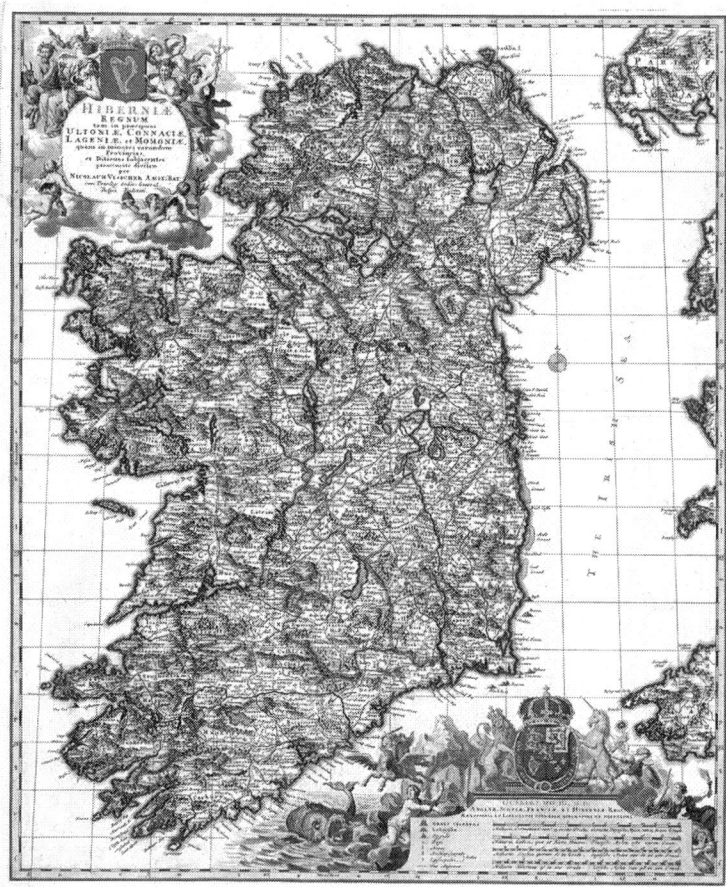

The Partition of Ireland

"The Honorable Member must remember that in the South they boasted of a Catholic State. They still boast of Southern Ireland being a Catholic State. All I boast of is that we are a Protestant Parliament and a Protestant State. It would be rather interesting for historians of the future to compare a Catholic State launched in the South with a Protestant State launched in the North and to see which gets on the better and prospers the more." – Sir James Craig

There are very few national relationships quite as complicated and enigmatic as the one that exists between the English and the Irish. For two peoples so interconnected by geography and history, the depth of animosity that is often expressed is difficult at times to understand. At the same time, historic links of family and clan, and common Gaelic roots, have at times fostered a degree of mutual regard, interdependence, and cooperation that is also occasionally hard to fathom.

During World War I, for example, Ireland fought for the British Empire as part of that empire, and the Irish response to the call to arms was at times just as enthusiastic as that of other British dominions such as Canada, Australia, and New Zealand. An excerpt from one war recruitment poster asked, "What have you done for Ireland? How have you answered the Call? Are you pleased with the part you're playing in the job that demands us all? Have you changed the tweed for the khaki to serve with rank and file, as your comrades are gladly serving, or isn't it worth your while?" And yet, at the same time, plots were unearthed to cooperate with the Germans in toppling British rule in Ireland, which would have virtually ensured an Allied defeat. In World War II, despite Irish neutrality, 12,000 Irish soldiers volunteered to join the Khaki line, returning after the war to the scorn and vitriol of a great many of their more radical countrymen.

One of the most bitter and divisive struggles in the history of the British Isles, and in the history of the British Empire, played out over the question of Home Rule and Irish independence, and then later still as the British province of Northern Ireland grappled within itself for the right to secede from the United Kingdom or the right to remain.

What is it within this complicated relationship that has kept this strange duality of mutual love and hate at play? A rendition of "Danny Boy" has the power to reduce both Irishmen and Englishmen to tears, and yet they have torn at one another in a violent conflict that can be traced to the very dawn of their contact.

This history of the British Isles themselves is in part responsible.[1] The fraternal difficulties of two neighbors so closely aligned, but so unequally endowed, can be blamed for much of the trouble. The imperialist tendencies of the English themselves, tendencies that created an empire that embodied the best and worst of humanity, alienated them from not only the Irish, but the Scots and Welsh too. However, the British also extended that colonial duality to other great societies of the world, India not least among them, without the same enduring suspicion and hostility. There is certainly something much more than the sum of its parts in this curious combination of love and loathing that characterizes the Anglo-Irish relationship.

The Partition of Ireland and the Troubles: The History of Northern Ireland from the Irish Civil War to the Good Friday Agreement analyzes the tumultuous events that marked the creation of Northern Ireland, and the conflicts fueled by the partition. Along with pictures of important people, places, and events, you will learn about Northern Ireland like never before.

.

---

[1] The *British Isles* consist of the islands of Great Britain, Ireland and over six thousand smaller isles and islands.

The Partition of Ireland and the Troubles: The History of Northern Ireland from the Irish Civil War to the Good Friday Agreement

About Charles River Editors

Introduction

    The Anglo-Irish Treaty

    The Irish Republic

    The Ulsters and Sectarian Violence

    The Beginning of the Troubles

    Bloody Sunday

    The Violence Continues

    Hunger Strikes and Political Prisoners

    The Peace Process

    Online Resources

    Bibliography

Free Books by Charles River Editors

Discounted Books by Charles River Editors

The Anglo-Irish Treaty

"When we have done our best, we can, as a united people, take whatever may befall us with quiet courage and confidence and this old nation will survive and if death should come to many of us, death is not the end." – Éamon de Valera

The Irish Home Rule Act had come into effect in 1914, two years after its successful passage through the British House of Commons. However, with the outbreak of war in Europe, the terms of the bill were immediately suspended, and Irish Home Rule was once again denied. The Irish, therefore, entered the war allied to the Triple Entente as a constituent territory of the British Empire, and a rush to recruitment began. In general, both unionists and republicans supported the war effort, and Irishmen flocked to the ranks, fighting in both the British and American armies.

On the other hand, the militant republican wing took the view that this snatching of Irish independence away at the moment that it was due was simply more evidence of British duplicity, and to them, this became fair grounds for the organization of a rebellion.

The Irish Volunteers and the more secretive Irish Republican Brotherhood then went about actively opposing enlistment while at the same time preparing the ground for an armed uprising. The Irish Republican Brotherhood was the main organizing body, but the largest body of active rebels came from the ranks of the Irish Volunteers, backed up by the Irish Citizen Army, then led by 48-year-old Roman Catholic nationalist James Connolly. Several hundred women were also directly involved, mostly members of Cumann na mBan, the concurrent Irish league of women. Action was to be coordinated by a seven-man Irish Republican Brotherhood military council drawn from each of the active organizations.

Connolly

The uprising was planned in utmost secrecy, in respect of the growing competence of the British intelligence services, and for the most part the necessary secrecy was achieved. The rationale behind the timing of the uprising was that England's difficulty was Ireland's opportunity. The Battle of Verdun was underway, and the Battle of the Somme was about to commence. The former was a largely French operation, but the Somme would be one of the worst bloodbaths of the war. It was also true that the nationalist revolutionary leadership was taken somewhat by surprise by the Irish Parliamentary Party position, and John Redmond's ready offer of assistance for the war effort. They may also have been shocked by the comprehensive response of Irish men to join the fight on behalf of the British. There was a sense within the nationalist movement that popular fervor for the cause might be waning, and indeed it was.

It was agreed by the military council, led by hardliner Padraig Pearse, that the rebellion would begin on Monday, April 24, 1916. The date happened to be Easter Monday.

Once the dust had settled and the island returned largely to civilian rule, a royal commission of inquiry was authorized to look into the causes of the rebellion. However, except for some mild criticism of the government in Dublin, nothing of any particular substance emerged. Within the city, in the aftermath of the whole messy business, the population was divided. It was generally agreed that the uprising had been sprung on them, and that there simply had been no time to take sides. The rebel position in the aftermath was simply that a military victory over the British had never really been possible, and that as a grand gesture to arouse the republican sentiments of the population, and to discredit the Irish Parliamentary Party, it had been a success. There was probably a strong measure of making a virtue out of a necessity in these proclamations, but in fact the ramifications of the Easter Rising certainly did begin to align the republican movement in Ireland in the direction of independence.

Obviously, historical analysis of the Easter Rising varies depending on the position of the observer, but in general it is understood that the 15 executions were foolish. James Connolly, wounded during the action, was strapped to a chair to be shot. The pathos of such an end certainly did deify him and many of his fellow martyrs, and the fact that all 15 died with their commitment undiminished simply added luster to their growing revolutionary legacy.

Roger Casement, who had already been convicted of treason before the Easter Rising and was waiting to be hanged, appealed on the eve of his execution for his countrymen to hold true to the struggle, writing, "If it be treason to fight against such an unnatural fate as this, then I am proud to be a rebel, and shall cling to my 'rebellion' with the last drop of my blood." Casement was hanged in August 1916, months after the uprising.

The 15 might have been regarded as casualties of impulse and the passion of the moment, but Casement's execution was seen simply as vindictive and reactionary. It was therefore as much the actions of the British as the Irish rebels that began to turn a majority of Irish in the direction of nationalism, and thoroughly against Britain. It also signaled a shift in approach from constitutional nationalism to revolutionary nationalism, and that was a dangerous precedent. Irish representation in the British Parliament, although satisfying and useful in some areas, had simply created a crop of moderate Irish Parliamentarians, the English regard for whom had been revealed when the modest gains of Home Rule were swept aside at the moment World War I diverted public attention.

French

In the closing phases of the war, conscription had been extended to Ireland, and the effect was galvanizing. Sinn Fein, the Irish Party, the Catholic hierarchy and various trades unions, all united by Éamon de Valera, the leader of Sinn Fein, rallied to oppose it. Nothing could more effectively have legitimized Sinn Fein than this demonstration of leadership of solidarity.

Éamon de Valera

Éamon de Valera was a seminal figure in the Irish march to independence that followed the Easter Rising. He was born in 1882 in New York to an Irish mother and a Spanish father, but from the age of 2, he lived with his parents in Ireland, and he became an early activist in the Home Rule and republican movement. He was a key organizer and participant in the Easter Rising, saved from execution only by the fact that he had been born in the United States. His subsequent prison term was not lengthy, although he was not released in time to stand as a Sinn Fein Party candidate in the 1918 election, during which he retained his seat. During that election, Sinn Fein took a majority of Irish seats outside of Ulster (73 of 105 Irish seats), but then refused to take those seats. Instead, an independent Irish Parliament was established, the Dáil Éireann, of which de Valera was elected president.

Members of the First Dáil

A studious, well-educated character, de Valera's early militant republicanism evolved into what has been described as social and cultural conservatism, and he remained Ireland's dominant political personality until his death in 1975.

During the period after the Easter Rising and World War I, as de Valera was gaining his political foothold, another powerful personality was also on the rise. Michael Collins was born in 1890 to a family with deep republican roots, stretching back to the rebellion of 1798. He was an English-trained lawyer, a tall and muscular man, conspicuously handsome, and highly intelligent. He had been a participant in the Easter Rising, and he too had served a short term of imprisonment, after which he began to rise rapidly through the ranks of the Irish Volunteers and Sinn Fein. As de Valera began his term as the president of the first Dáil, Collins joined him as Minister of Finance.

Michael Collins in 1919 as Minister of Finance

24 Sinn Fein members (the rest were imprisoned, among them de Valera himself) gathered on January 21, 1919 for the inaugural meeting of the Dáil, which established a government for Ireland and implemented an independent judicial system along with various government departments.[2] It was unable to entirely control the emerging Irish Republican Army, still loyal to its roots in the Irish Republican Brotherhood. While de Valera presided over the political institutions of an independent Ireland, Collins became increasingly engaged in what was soon to be known as the "War of Independence."

The founding of the Dáil Éireann marked a turning point in the popular perception of the process that was now underway. Under the noses of the British, a movement to establish the fundamentals of independence was taking place, in a manner that would not only be recognized

---

[2] The Unionists and the Irish Parliamentary Party ignored the summons to the Dáil.

by the British, but which also won much international sympathy. In the aftermath of its founding, the Irish Republican Brotherhood began to be referred to increasingly as the "Irish Republican Army," or the IRA. Before that, the notion of armed action had taken the form of an uprising configured on the hope of a general insurrection to follow, but the IRA began to work along the lines of an asymmetric war. A new leadership began employing guerrilla tactics that were less easy to suppress in a single police action, and which developed into a state of general insecurity that aimed to make Ireland largely ungovernable by the British.

The IRA staged its first action in breaking de Valera out of Lincoln Prison, as well as fellow nationalists Sean McGarry and Sean Mulroy. The operation was carried out on February 4, 1919 by Michael Collins, along with colleagues Harry Boland and Frank Kelly. It was a daring and successful operation, offering a boost in confidence to a militant wing by then accustomed to brutal defeat. De Valera remained in hiding for several weeks after the breakout, but a government amnesty published in March allowed him to return to Dublin, and in April he was formally inducted into the presidency of the Dáil.

Coinciding with the January 21 founding of the Dáil, the first shots were fired in what came to be known as Anglo-Irish War, or the War of Independence. A group from the 3rd Tipperary Brigade of the IRA ambushed two members of the Royal Irish Constabulary who were escorting a consignment of gelignite explosives to Soloheadbeg, County Tipperary. The two officers were killed and the explosives seized. Operations then began on a regular, but fairly limited scale, until by 1920, as the IRA gathered in confidence, offensive actions were becoming better coordinated and a great deal deadlier. Tactics developed by the Boer in South Africa were modified and adapted to conditions in Ireland, and the effect in general was profound. Ambushes, hit-and-run attacks, snipers, and the use of flying columns all challenged the capacity of the British, who responded with a campaign of night raids, widespread searches, random arrests, and shootings. It was a bloody conflict of attrition, but the British were at least robbed of the quick and decisive victory to which they had for so long become accustomed.

Along with his government functions, in which he proved to be an exceptional finance official, Michael Collins was also Director of Organization and President of the Supreme Council of the Irish Republican Brotherhood. His operations room was the bar at Vaughan's Hotel in Central Dublin, and from there he controlled and coordinated the various regional cells and chapters of the IRA. Under the nose of the British, he ran this campaign, earning the moniker the Irish Scarlet Pimpernel. His style was cavalier, and while he appeared to court risk, he was shrewd, intuitive, and enormously courageous.

In May 1919, as Collins ran the armed campaign, de Valera set off for the United States to campaign for the Irish Republic, aware that the British had to take another international power's opinion into account for the first time in modern history. Indeed, the imperial complexion of Europe had shifted dramatically since the end of the war. The German, Russian and Ottoman

Empires no longer existed, and under the aegis of the newly minted League of Nations, numerous liberated territories were governed under international mandates. The British Empire, still mostly intact and actually larger thanks to the mandates that it had been granted, had nonetheless been served notice that the days of international empires were drawing quickly to a close. The principal constituents of the empire were already beginning to reformulate their relationship with Britain in the direction of a commonwealth, and the American position was on the whole anti-imperial.

It was uncomfortable, naturally, for the British to observe the tour de force of an Irish statesman of the quality of de Valera in a nation where Irish influence was huge and growing. The outcome of the Easter Rising, with all of its imagery of David and Goliath, and the executions of the 15 martyrs, had engendered widespread and deep sympathy in the United States, even among groups not traditionally engaged in Irish affairs.

By this time, the British political establishment had grown somewhat less averse to the idea of an independent Ireland, but the loud minority of Ulster Unionists continued to declare British or Die, and the threat of a civil war remained undiminished. In the end, the British needed to figure out a way to deal with a simmering, low-level war within Ireland, and a great deal of moral pressure from across the Atlantic. To that end, the British governing establishment, still dominated by Prime Minister David Lloyd George, produced the 1920 Government of Ireland Act. This not only recognized the Irish Parliament, or the Dáil, but also granted a second Parliament in the north, serving the separate interests of the Unionists.

David Lloyd George

   This was the first formal intimation of partition as a solution to the deepening Catholic/Protestant split in Ireland. Ireland was divided into 26 counties in the south and 6 in the north, each given de facto home rule, with the former governed from Dublin and the latter from Belfast. The Unionists reluctantly approved this, primarily because it sheltered the north from any immediate absorption into the south, though a Council of Ireland was implemented and added to the mix to plan and prepare the way for an eventual integration. Sinn Fein, on the other hand, rejected the terms of the Act outright, arguing that a grant of Parliamentary autonomy was moot because the Republic of Ireland had been in de facto existence since 1916. Michael Collins increased his military activity, and de Valera, once he returned from America, entered into immediate correspondence with David Lloyd George.

   What David Lloyd George had to offer was something less than a full republic. The organization of the empire was evolving in the direction of a commonwealth, or a federation of largely independent entities known as dominions. A dominion differed from a colony insofar as the latter was ruled directly from Whitehall via a governor or viceroy, with no independent institutions at all. This status was typically applied to a dependent territory deemed incapable of self-government, and such was the case with most of the African colonies, with the exception of South Africa. A self-governing colony, on the other hand, was a status somewhere in between. The dominions at that time were Canada, South Africa, Australia, and New Zealand. Ireland, for the moment, was ruled as a colony, as was India, and the reasons were the same. The dominions were populated and governed by predominately loyal subjects who were unlikely to rock the boat, but with the devolution of greater domestic authority to local institutions, India and Ireland would both tear away from the empire at the earliest opportunity.

It was, in essence, dominion status that David Lloyd George offered de Valera, with certain guarantees to ensure the retention of British trade interests, military cooperation, defense revenue, law and order, and police. De Valera, a staunch republican, could not bring himself to entertain anything less than a republic. Dominion status for Ireland, he maintained, was an illusion, which it was indeed. He further noted that a harmonious relationship between Dublin and London could only be achieved by complete independence and the establishment of a republic. As de Valera put it, "The sole cause of the ancient feuds, which you deplore, has been, as we know, and as history proves, the attacks of English rulers upon Irish liberties. These attacks can cease forthwith, if your Government has the will. The road to peace and understanding lies open."

These discussions took place via written correspondence, which initially commenced as open and cordial, but by the end had turned terse, economical, and at times combative. Prime Minister Lloyd George was a Welshman, and a master of misty obfuscation and vague determinations, whereas de Valera was an avid ideologue, impatient with diplomacy and gifted with very little humor. A face-to-face meeting was arranged only after Lloyd George, in his typically opaque way, was prepared to acknowledge the Irish delegation as representing a sovereign and free state, but he did so with his fingers firmly crossed behind his back.

The delegation selected to travel to London did not include de Valera himself, which is interesting since it implied either that he did not trust himself to be sufficiently pragmatic to strike a deal or that he did not wish to be associated with whatever deal would emerge. An uncompromising republican position would not prevail, and clearly he understood this. The delegation was instead led by Michael Collins, an entirely different type of character, and a brave choice. While undeniably violent and capable of making the difficult decisions expected of the leader of a guerrilla army, he was also charming and easy to get along with. His position might be expected to be as uncompromising as de Valera's, perhaps even more so, but in the end, he accepted and engineered a compromise, understanding very clearly the consequences of not doing so.

From the sidelines, de Valera might have sensed he made a mistake in placing Collins at the head of the delegation, for soon he was facing the entire panoply of the British inner cabinet. These included men like Winston Churchill and the Lord Chancellor, Lord Birkenhead, both notoriously prickly characters. It was Churchill who perhaps recognized most clearly the way things were inevitably going. He later wrote, "The choice was clearly open. Crush them with vain and unstinted force, or try to give them what they want. These were the only alternatives, and although each had ardent advocates, most people were unprepared for either. Here indeed was the specter, horrid and inexorcisable."

It is also worth noting that Churchill, with his famous wit and humor, although wary of the Irish on a political level, was extremely fond of them. He famously sparred with George Bernard Shaw, using the acerbic wit that both men perfected over their lifetimes. Michael Collins was precisely the type of Irishman that Churchill enjoyed the most; he was not to be trifled with, and he was ready to exchange rhetorical blows with the master. The two men bonded, in part in the interests of the game afoot, but also from a genuine sense of friendship and confederacy. Churchill's position, reflecting a consensus on his side of the floor, was that Irish links with Britain, in particular that of defense, would remain sacrosanct. As Collins occasionally backslid, Churchill would remind him that British military support for the troublesome Ulster Unionists was always a matter of priority.

A picture of Collins in London

The result of all of this was the Anglo-Irish treaty of 1921, and the terms of that treaty were that the British agreed to concede dominion status to the south, which would thereafter be known as the Irish Free State. The head of the dominion would remain the British king, represented in

Dublin by a governor general. The various office holders of government and the administration would take an oath of allegiance to the Crown. Three ports in the south would remain British territory for the purpose of imperial security, and Ireland would remain part of the British Commonwealth. For the remainder, southern Ireland would be practically independent, the role of the governor largely ceremonial and the oaths of allegiance nothing more than a formality, albeit a rather bitter one.

For many, this was a very difficult hurdle to leap, but Collins, exercising the pragmatism that few would have expected, argued that dominion status was simply a large step in the direction of full independence, and that in time, perhaps sooner rather than later, Ireland would win full independence. The alternative would be the "vain and unstinting force" referred to by Churchill, with the inevitable result of a retraction of the advances made since 1916.

In the end, it was an emotional and somewhat melodramatic ultimatum by Lloyd George that pushed the doubters to the table. Eventually, the various Irish delegates added their signatures to the agreement.

As for Northern Ireland, the 1921 treaty formalized partition, with the understanding that the two would merge again at some point. That said, it is debatable how seriously that understanding was taken. A clause was included that allowed for the north to separate entirely from the Irish Free State upon direct representation to the Crown, which it promptly did. The day after the establishment of the Irish Free State, more or less a year after the signing of the treaty, an address was delivered to the Crown: "Most Gracious Sovereign, We, your Majesty's most dutiful and loyal subjects, the Senators and Commons of Northern Ireland in Parliament assembled, having learnt of the passing of the Irish Free State Constitution Act 1922, being the Act of Parliament for the ratification of the Articles of Agreement for a Treaty between Great Britain and Ireland, do, by this humble Address, pray your Majesty that the powers of the Parliament and Government of the Irish Free State shall no longer extend to Northern Ireland."

The Irish Republic

"Think what I have got for Ireland. Something which she has wanted these past 700-years, will anybody be satisfied with this bargain? Will anyone? I tell you this, early this morning I signed my death warrant." - Michael Collins

Once the facts of the treaty had been digested at home, its implications almost immediately split the republican movement. The split ran broadly along the lines of support for Michael Collins or Éamon de Valera. Incompatible personalities to begin with, the two very quickly became irreconcilable. The de Valera faction expressed dismay that the delegates to London had signed off on a partitioned Ireland, and over the question of Ireland's constitutional status under the terms of the Irish Free State, they were completely incensed.

In a way, this was indicative of an emerging power struggle between the dour and intellectual de Valera and the populist Collins. Collins maintained, very practically, that what he had achieved was the best that could be achieved under the circumstances. The Lloyd George ultimatum threatened war if an agreement was not reached, and while an armed guerrilla movement in Ireland could bait and irritate the British, victory in an open war would be impossible. The IRA could induce the British to negotiate, but it stood no chance in an open conflict. Lloyd George would not force unity on the Ulster Unionists, nor would he tolerate an independent Irish republic. These were the simple facts. What Collins maintained he had done was not to win a republic for Ireland, but to secure her the opportunity to obtain it in the future. As he put it, the treaty earned Ireland "not the ultimate freedom that all nations aspire and develop to, but the freedom to achieve it."

Collins later gave voice to the popular suspicion that de Valera had sent him to negotiate with the British simply because he was aware of the probable outcome and did not wish to be directly identified with it. He claimed to have felt deeply betrayed when de Valera refused to stand by or endorse the agreement that Collins returned from London with, but for his part, de Valera felt the agreement had been sprung on him, and that the delegates had signed off on it without consultation with those at home which also was true.

Both men had plenty of followers, and the subsequent split in the republican movement saw many old friends and comrades divided over this issue. Despite this, when it was put to a vote on January 1922, the Dáil Éireann narrowly passed the Anglo-Irish Treaty, and thus it became law.

Following this, in accordance with Article 17 of the Treaty, the Provisional Government of the Irish Free State was established. De Valera promptly resigned as president of the republic, but failed in his reelection by a similarly narrow margin. He then challenged the right of the Dáil to approve the treaty, saying that its members were breaking their oath to the Irish Republic. His position thereafter remained intractably opposed to the treaty.

De Valera's stance was supported by many senior members of the IRA, who in March 1922 repudiated the authority of the Dáil to accept the treaty. Meanwhile, Collins worked to build a new National Army from pro-treaty elements in the IRA. Displaying once again the unexpected pragmatism of a natural politician, Collins was able to patch over differences and unite Sinn Fein and the IRA, the latter over a common interest in commencing operations against Northern Ireland.

The first general election in the Irish Free State was scheduled in June 1922, but just before the ballot, the two sides split once again over the inclusion of the British monarch in the Free State's constitution. Collins' pro-Treaty Sinn Fein won a majority of the seats, leading to a civil war that devolved into a bitter contest of erratic guerrilla attacks and retaliations. This led to more extrajudicial killings and executions, occasional pitched battles, and a great many retaliatory killings. It was an ugly and brutal affair, but by August 1922, the worst of it seemed to be over, with pro-treaty forces generally in the commanding position.

On August 22, 1922, Collins set out from the city of Cork to tour pro-treaty positions in West Cork. At an isolated crossroads known as Béal na Bláth, his party paused to question a man standing there. The man proved to be an anti-treaty sentry, and he and an associate immediately recognized Collins seated in the back of an open-topped car. A group of anti-treaty militants quickly formed an ambush at the crossroads, anticipating correctly that the convoy of cars carrying Collins would return by the same route. When it did, the ambush was sprung, and in the ensuing firefight, Collins was shot dead.

A picture of Collins' funeral

Michael Collins' assassination has intrigued historians and conspiracy theorists ever since. Although no evidence exists to support the theory, there are many who believe that de Valera was directly implicated in the arrangement of the ambush, and even of drawing Collins into the kill zone. The basis of these theories are the anecdotal reports and reflections of various officers on both sides, but firm evidence to support the assertion is entirely absent.

Ultimately, anti-treaty forces were compelled to surrender in May 1923, and the divided sides eventually amalgamated to form the progenitors of Ireland's future political parties, Fine Gael and the Fianna Fáil.

Between 1924 and 1925, a Boundary Commission met to establish the new borders of Northern

Ireland. The commission was headed by Justice Richard Feetham of South Africa, Eoin MacNeill representing the Irish Free State and Joseph R. Fisher representing Northern Ireland. Both sides observed keenly the progress of the commission, although in respect of likely controversy, the details and findings were kept secret. Press leaks stirred up considerable anxiety on both sides, and in the end, existing borders were more or less confirmed, with only very minor adjustments. Parts of Fermanagh, Tyrone, and Armagh were ceded to the Irish Free State and a part of Donegal to Northern Ireland. Beyond that, not much changed. Northern Ireland remained comprised of the six counties of Antrim, Armagh, Down, Fermanagh, Londonderry (Derry), and Tyrone, and the balance remained the Irish Free State.

Inevitably, even these minor adjustments antagonized both sides. One of the problems of Irish partition, a problem that would be replicated on a much vaster scale in India in 1947, was the residual populations of Protestants in Southern Ireland and Catholics in Northern Ireland. As for the former, most eventually made their way to Northern Ireland, but the half a million or so nationalist Catholics who remained in Northern Ireland did not relocate, and they remained steadfastly unreconciled to the dispensation of government and territory. Moreover, they suffered real discrimination in terms of employment, public housing, education, and social services. Roman Catholic representation, already compromised, was further limited by creative electoral boundary delineation.

All of this was compensated for somewhat by steady and robust economic growth in the north which was not replicated in the south in any meaningful way. On the eve of partition, Belfast was the largest city in Ireland, with a population of over 350,000, and with a strong employment market in textiles. The city also boasted a massive shipbuilding industry. Protestants were overrepresented in skilled jobs and managerial positions, but there was still enough to go around, and Catholics were incentivized to stay. In conjunction with that, poor Catholics from the south were attracted to come to Northern Ireland for employment opportunities.

Sectarian violence was a fact of life, and housing was heavily segregated, with Catholics in general occupying slum areas. The Great Depression was more keenly felt in the south than the north, especially as the threat of another European war approached. Thanks to the rising tension, Northern Ireland's shipbuilding and other industries boomed as a result of European rearmament. Catholics did not abandon the opportunity-rich north, but at the same time, the sharp inequalities of Northern Ireland bred deep antipathies that threatened future difficulties.

To the south, the Irish Free State settled into its existence. The elements of an independent republic were constitutionally absent, but in practical terms, as with every colony of the empire endowed with responsible government, de facto independence existed in every form other than name. As Michael Collins had observed, the Anglo-Irish Treaty provided the freedom to achieve freedom. Indeed, Irish freedom as it stood in 1925 exceeded anything achieved in the four centuries prior, and Ireland was indeed, for all intents and purposes, independent. A functioning, if somewhat rancorous and disputed parliamentary democracy existed, with an independent executive and judiciary, all of which certainly exceeded the stated goals of the Home Rule.

However, what did not exist was constitutional separation from England, which meant the visceral desire at the heart of the Irish protest was not answered. For example, the British monarch remained the monarch of Ireland, and legislation passed through the Irish Parliament was subject to Royal Assent, or what was informally known as the imperial veto. This required the submission of approved bills for the further approval of the Colonial Office. It was for the most part a formality, but any attempt by either house to abolish the oath would have been guaranteed a veto.

Even as some in Ireland chafed, changes within the British imperial structure that began after World War I steadily loosened the bonds of imperial control over the various dominions, and the movement towards independence was certainly not limited to Ireland. Periodic imperial conferences were held in London, where the prime ministers of the various dominions met to discuss imperial policy. During the 1926 Imperial Conference, it was declared that all member states of the Commonwealth would be equal, and a reform was implemented that altered the title of the monarch to By the Grace of God, of Great Britain, Ireland and the British Dominions beyond the Seas King, Defender of the Faith, Emperor of India.

The Irish Free State did not toe the line quite so obediently as the other dominions, and it went over the head of the British in accepting credentials from foreign diplomats. Then, in 1931, the Statute of Westminster was enacted, which further loosened the paternal bonds of empire. The imperial veto was abandoned, which, in de jure terms, made the dominions sovereign territories, disengaged in every sense other than ceremonial from political obligations to the British. The test of this was in foreign policy, and in 1931, the Irish Free State negotiated an independent treaty with Portugal and passed an independent act of Parliament recognizing the abdication of King Edward VIII. The Great Seal of the Realm was replaced by the Great Seal of Saorstát Éireann, which was awarded to the Irish Free State by the king in 1931.

In 1932, Éamon de Valera was elected to the office of Prime Minister of the Irish Free State, and one of his first actions was to abolish the Irish oath of allegiance to the British Crown, as well as other precepts, including appeals to the Privy Council. The Privy Council acted as an advisory body in affairs of the empire, from which Ireland now excluded itself. In 1937, the Irish Free State eradicated any and all references to the British Crown from its constitution, other than allowing the king to act on behalf of Ireland in foreign affairs, but soon afterwards this too was expunged. The country was renamed Eire.

This effectively brought the Irish Free State to an end. With the rise of militarism in Europe and a decreased threat of German mischief in Ireland, nothing was done in Whitehall to obstruct this. The situation was summed up rather succinctly by the Irish academic Thomas Desmond Williams, who wrote, "By the time the British had found the answer, the Irish had lost interest in the question."

In 1949, Eire assumed the name of the Irish Republic and withdrew from the British Commonwealth.

The Ulsters and Sectarian Violence

The affairs of Ireland during the months and years following the Anglo-Irish Treaty of 1921 were driven by almost entirely by the Ulster Loyalist determination to remain part of the British Empire. The British government supported this, aware that even if it had an inclination to do so, it would be extremely ill-advised to force the Protestant communities of Northern Ireland to do anything they did not want to do.

While Michael Collins and Éamon de Valera largely drove the Republican agenda, the Unionist leader was Sir James Craig, 1st Viscount Craigavon. Son of a wealthy distiller, Craig had served in the Royal Irish Rifles, and he had seen action in the Boer War. He was a man of average height, but well-set, bull-necked, and powerful. Provided with independent means, he entered politics, representing the constituency of East Down from 1906-1918, and from 1918-1921 that of Mid Down. He also held two official government positions in the British administration, those being Parliamentary Secretary to the Minister for Pensions and Parliamentary Secretary to the Admiralty.

Craig

While somewhat less militant than his southern Irish counterparts, it was Craig who was largely responsible for raising the Ulster Volunteers, the first paramilitary organization in Northern Ireland, and he facilitated the purchase of arms and ammunition from Imperial Germany. In February 1921, in the Northern Ireland General Election, the first of its kind to be held, he entered the Parliament of Northern Ireland as Member for County Down. Soon afterwards, he was appointed first Prime Minister of Northern Ireland by the Lord Lieutenant of Ireland.[3]

On January 23, 1922, about six months before his assassination, Michael Collins and Sir James Craig met in London to formalize casual discussions that had been ongoing for some time. The result of this was the signing of what came to be known as the Craig-Collins Pact of 1922, the signing of which pleasantly surprised a great many people on both sides of the partition line. The agreement covered issues such as a revised Boundary Commission, an end to a southern trade boycott of the north, an agreement that Catholics would receive fairer treatment in the north, the replacement of the Council of Ireland as the body dealing with pan-Irish affairs, and a

---

[3] Unionist opposition to Home Rule had been led by Edward Carson, Northern Irish barrister and judge.

commitment to make progress over the release of political prisoners. It was all very cordial, and suitably vague, marking a rare moment of rapprochement that few on either side would have anticipated.

Craig, however, had been made aware through contacts with British intelligence that on the eve of the Anglo-Irish truce in July 1921, the IRA was intending to infiltrate 500 men into Northern Ireland to commence guerrilla warfare. He made overtures to Collins over the matter, dealing not specifically with this threat, but attempting to diffuse any future aggressive action by the IRA by showing a willingness to meet and compromise. Collins was precisely the man to approach, and the discussions that followed, tentative initially, yielded a signed accord. For his part, Collins, while no less a diehard nationalist, was also aware that a majority of Irish, after the traumatic events of the Civil War, had no appetite for another bout of de facto warfare. He was also very concerned about the release of IRA prisoners.

News of the signing of this pact triggered a bout of press speculation that in the end proclaimed this moment as the first stepping stone towards a future of mutual cooperation between the north and the south. According to Craig himself, "For the credit of our land we were able to put our joint names to a document which…is an admission by the Free State that Ulster is an entity of its own, with a head with whom they can, at any rate, confer…" Craig was a staunch Protestant and a loyal Orangeman, but he was not quite as unyielding as many on either side who were busy creating the ground rules for a divided Ireland. Like Michael Collins, while standing firmly in his own corner, he was quite able to cast a pragmatic eye over the battlefield.

There was, however, some hubris when it came to Craig's reaction to the signing. Michael Collins, after all, offered no public recognition to Northern Ireland, and he did not recognize the Craig regime. The Boundary Commission was yet to meet, and its findings had not been reached, so there was much to be hoped for from the outcome on both sides.

On June 22, 1922 King George V officially opened the Northern Ireland Parliament, making formal use for the first time of the term "Six Counties" in reference to Northern Ireland. This, in the ears of some alert members, implied that the Six Counties were somehow de facto.

By then, the findings of the Boundary Commission had been made public, and sidestepping an obvious hot political potato, it opted to simply recommend no real change at all. Those anticipating a radical revision of the Six Counties border in favor of the south were to be disappointed. In 1921, the republican determination to achieve a unified republic, including the six counties, had been softened only by assurances from the British that the Boundary Commission would return counties Fermanagh and Tyrone. This would immediately render Northern Ireland inviable as a stand-alone territory, and it would collapse.

By this time, violent incursions in Northern Ireland had begun, and a local IRA presence in Northern Ireland was established. At the same time, the IRA was conducting violent actions outside of Northern Ireland as well. On May 25, 1921, the Customs House in Dublin was occupied and then destroyed in an IRA operation. The operation involved over 100 IRA paramilitaries, and although it proved to be a significant propaganda coup for the republicans, it was not a conspicuous military success. A force of British Auxiliaries quickly arrived on the scene, and a major gun battle erupted, during which five IRA combatants were killed and several more were captured. A small handful managed to slip away and merge with the civilian Catholic community. This was one of the first major IRA actions in Northern Ireland, and it was certainly a sign of things to come.

A picture of the Customs House on fire

Northern Irish Catholics were a strong minority in the partitioned Northern Ireland, and they formed majorities of the population in most of the rural west and many districts in the city of Belfast. Thanks to heavy industry, a great many industrial workers were housed in certain specific districts of the city, all of which had for a long time been highly militant cantonments virtually off limits to the Protestant-dominated population. There was no lack of incentive to resort to violence, and the IRA provided the vehicle. On both sides of the partition line, therefore, the campaign of violence accelerated.

In response to IRA actions, loyalist violence against Catholics rose quickly in frequency and severity, and the violence spread to mainland England. On June 22, 1922, Field Marshal Sir

Henry Hughes Wilson, one of the most senior British officers in World War I, and very briefly an Irish Unionist politician, was gunned down in London by two IRA volunteers. It was a messy operation, targeting Sir Wilson as he returned home from unveiling the Great Eastern Railway War Memorial erected at Liverpool Street station. Two police officers accompanying him and a chauffeur were also shot as the two IRA men attempted to evade capture. Both assailants were quickly surrounded by a crowd of onlookers and arrested after a struggle. Soon afterwards, they appeared in court, were convicted of murder, and hanged on August 10, 1922.

Wilson

Thereafter, violence in Northern Ireland became a fact of life. The frontline of the conflict soon enough settled on the city of Belfast, capital city of Northern Ireland, and of course, a city with a working Catholic community. Between July 1920 and July 1922, a total of 636 killings were recorded in Northern Ireland, 460 of which took place in Belfast. Of these, 258 were Catholic, despite the fact that Catholics made up less than a quarter of the population of the city.

After 1923, as the provisions of the Anglo-Irish Treaty began to be put into effect, violence diminished somewhat. The situation was dealt with by the civil authorities under the Emergency Powers Act (Northern Ireland), while the unenviable task of frontline enforcement fell to the much-storied Royal Ulster Constabulary. The Royal Ulster Constabulary was formed on June 1, 1922, a continuation of the soon to be defunct Royal Irish Constabulary. A handful of Catholics were transferred from the Royal Irish Constabulary to the Royal Ulster Constabulary, but in general very few Catholics signed up for service, and the RUC was identified as a largely Protestant force throughout the conflict. Many Irish nationalists in Northern Ireland took the view that the RUC was a sectarian force, which in certain divisions it was, all of which simply added to the growing Catholic sense of isolation.

In the aftermath of the establishment of Northern Ireland, both the territory and its government were left largely to their own devices. The findings of the Boundary Commission tended to nullify the Craig-Collins Pact, and under successive Unionist Prime Ministers, a pattern of discrimination against Catholics throughout the territory became steadily more institutionalized. This was most blatant in the manipulation of voter districts to ensure that areas of Catholic majorities were added to electoral wards where their majority would be eclipsed by a Unionist majority. Voter qualifications were set high enough to limit as many Catholics as possible, a well-seasoned system throughout the empire that remained in force in Northern Ireland until 1969, despite having been abolished on the mainland by 1940.

A tapering system of proportional representation certainly delivered some parity in Parliament for the Catholic minority, finally falling away in 1929, giving the dominant Ulster Union Party a de facto one-party rule status that endured for nearly 50 years.

Discrimination in terms of political representation, although a source of deep resentment, was not quite so keenly felt as anti-Catholic discrimination in the workplace. This was no less blatant, and a great deal more impactful. Northern Ireland at that time was home to one of Europe's largest shipbuilding industries, alongside a great many other branches of manufacturing and heavy engineering, and job discrimination tended to keep Catholics out of the higher management and executive positions.

There was, however, a robust market in industrial labor, which kept Catholics in Belfast and attracted many more. The Northern Irish economy boomed during this period, especially in the years after World War II, which meant that Catholic workers in Northern Ireland tended to still be in a better position than their southern Irish counterparts.

Sectarian violence, after having diminished slightly since its peak in 1922, erupted again in 1935. Throughout the spring and summer of that year, a vicious campaign of sectarian violence had been steadily building in and around Belfast, and matters came to a head on the "Glorious Twelfth" of July, long celebrated to commemorate the Glorious Revolution of 1688. On July 12, 1935, a Protestant Orange Order parade was routed provocatively close to a Catholic area. The resulting violence left nine people dead and scores injured.[4]

A report on the incident was filed by civil rights campaigner Ronald Kidd for the National Council of Civil Liberties, based in London. Kidd was at the time chairman of the influential NCCL, and he visited Belfast during the worst of the violence. He wrote, "At a riot on June 12 – at which I was present – following an inflammatory meeting of the Ulster Protestant League at the Customs House steps, an unruly mob of some thousands of men and women swept through the business quarter of the city. Men, not all of them sober, were dancing in the ranks and women were screaming as they marched. I pointed out to a constable that this was an illegal assembly at common law. The mob were getting out of hand; and as they reached York Street, they ran completely amok. A bomb was thrown into a shop; shots were fired; every window in the Labour Club was broken, and Catholic shop-windows along York Street were smashed in with stones and iron bolts. One arrest was made, but the prisoner was rescued by the mob. We are justified in asking (a) why this dangerous mob, which was visibly out for riot, was allowed by the police to proceed on its way; (b) why nine armoured cars and hundreds of armed police were unable to effect even the one arrest which they attempted; (c) why this force of armed police were unable to prevent wholesale riot and damage."

On the eve of World War II, the IRA launched "S-Plan," a bombing and sabotage campaign against the English mainland that occurred between 1939 and 1940. There were numerous sabotage attempts made, with most either failing or being foiled, but a number of successful detonations occurred in London and elsewhere. Upon the declaration of war, Northern Ireland was automatically drawn into the conflict on the Allies' side, while Ireland remained neutral.

Ireland did not entirely escape the war unscathed. Four German air raids were recorded over Belfast in the spring of 1941, targeting mainly military and manufacturing facilities. Lighter raids also targeted Dublin and a few Irish ports. De Valera voiced his opposition to the stationing of American troops in Northern Ireland, where they were billeted as part of the spread of American personnel across the British Isles.

Besides that, Northern Ireland remained largely peaceful, with little if any organized sectarian violence in the period during and immediately after the war. The declaration of an Irish republic went ahead, and the Republic of Ireland officially came into being in 1949.

The Beginning of the Troubles

"To gain what is worth having, it may be necessary to lose everything." – Bernadette Devlin

The first orchestrated series of attacks in the post-war period began in December 1956, in what was codenamed "Operation Harvest," but more widely known as the "Border Campaign." This was a series of guerrilla operations staged throughout Northern Ireland, focusing mainly in the border areas before winding down in early 1962. As with most similar operations, Operation

---

[4] The "Glorious Twelfth" is the date upon which members of the Orange Order celebrate the Battle of the Boyne in 1690, that began the Protestant Ascendancy in Northern Ireland.

Harvest was relatively easily contained by the RUC, and as a military operation, it is accepted that it was a failure. However, under the principle that an army cannot be idle, it did keep the combatant core of the IRA occupied and interested at a low point in the organization's history. When dwindling support brought the operation to a close, the IRA went underground.

On the other side, the Ulster Volunteer Force was formed in May 1966. This was a separate, but parallel organization to the UVF of a century earlier. This was a seminal moment in the sequence of events in Northern Ireland, adding an additional dimension to organized violence in Ulster. The organization was founded as a Unionist paramilitary defense against the IRA, and if the IRA was violent, the UVF was extremely so. Even worse, it was initially less disciplined and more poorly led than the IRA. Most of its victims were Irish Catholic civilians targeted for real or perceived links with the IRA, or simply as random targets of retaliation. The UVF also took on a vigilante law and order role in working-class communities, acting in this role with no reduction in violence at all.

In 1971, a second Unionist paramilitary group, the Ulster Defense Association, came into being. It was dedicated to precisely the same cause as the UFV, and it deployed similar tactics. By then, under the administration of Prime Minister Captain Terence O'Neill, there was observed to be a state of de facto "apartheid" in Northern Ireland. This accusation was hard to refute in the face of the stark lines of separation quite evident between Catholic and Protestant communities all over the land. This separation was even more acutely noticeable in light of the conspicuous impoverishment of Catholic areas of Northern Ireland. Terence O'Neill argued that this situation was organic, and that in a modern context, sectarian differences made no difference at all. The rise of a Catholic middle class tended to reflect this, although it did not speak for the working majority of Catholics.

The situation in Northern Ireland began to deteriorate as the 1960s progressed, and it descended into virtual anarchy by 1968. For this, many reasons have been suggested. For example, highly educated young Catholic graduates began to emerge from local and overseas universities in increasing numbers and began to agitate for better access to jobs and housing. More radical groups were inspired by the American Civil Rights Movement, and they were empowered by both education and the growing liberation theology of the times.[5]

During the decade, the IRA as a militant organization had languished, steadily reduced by disinterest and an ongoing internal squabble over whether radical politics or armed force represented the best vehicle for real change. This was deeply unsatisfactory to a new generation, certainly to the students and graduates, but also to young Catholics growing up in the north. By 1967, however, Northern Ireland Catholics were demanding immediate change, and their demands were becoming louder and more insistent.

---

[5] The 1960s saw most African territories achieve independence from their European colonial masters, and in South Africa and the United States, strong movements of educated and radicalized black youth challenged the status quo.

One such graduate was 20-year-old Roman Catholic Bernadette Devlin, a civil rights activist who led numerous demonstrations in Belfast in support of fair representation, equal housing allocations, and an end to voting inequalities. Many of these activities were deliberately provocative. In 1968, for example, Devlin and other radical young student leaders led a series of marches intended to incite the Orange Order. The Orange Order, a Protestant fraternal order, stood on a radically opposing platform, and was usually alert to any opportunity to demonstrate to that effect. The language of the Catholic civil rights movement in Northern Ireland was radically tinged and rather fearsome in the age of a "Red under the bed" Cold War context, stirring a visceral indignation in Protestant militant circles. It naturally attracted official condemnation – the students were condemned as "republican" under different flags – which had the effect of alerting elements in the moribund IRA to the potential for radical politics as an alternative to an unwinnable war.

Kenneth Allen's picture of a mural depicting Devlin

Devlin was typical of many radical young Catholics of the period. She ruffled many feathers by speaking both candidly and loudly, and she produced incendiary political tracts and publications of heavily left-leaning ideology. In the aftermath of the 1969 general election, she narrowly secured the Parliamentary seat for Mid Ulster. At just 21, she was the youngest sitting member of the British House of Commons, and with precocious confidence, she took her oath of allegiance and an hour later commenced her maiden speech.

All of this was extremely inspiring to young Catholics, who were Bernadette Devlin's natural constituency, but it did nothing to satisfy the narrow clique of hard-line republicans still in the IRA. They were the radicalized cadre, ideologically allied to Marxist guerrilla groups springing up all over Europe, as well as others like the Palestinian Liberation Organization. In common with them all, these members of the IRA had no interest in Parliaments and puppet governments. There was a strong movement within the IRA to return to positive action, and while Devlin's seat on the backbenches in Westminster ignited a strong political movement, the radicals in the IRA were keenly waiting for the spark that would reignite the armed struggle.

For its part, the Royal Ulster Constabulary, an instinctively unionist institution, but also the agent of law and order, had very little sympathy for the growing Catholic civil rights movement. That movement did not go out of its way to make friends with the police, so the RUC tended to deploy the stick more frequently than any carrot. The RUC was not overtly partisan, and it performed with the same professionalism as any other branch of the British police, but tensions between the two sides were extremely high, and everything came to a head in a seminal event known as the Battle of the Bogside.

The Battle of the Bogside took place in Londonderry from August 12-14, 1969. Londonderry, now known as Derry, was a majority Catholic city that was governed, through electoral district gerrymandering, by the Ulster Unionist Party. The city was also, quite naturally, a strong center for Catholic civil rights activism. In the summer of 1969, tensions in the city were high, and the population was deeply polarized. Ongoing sectarian clashes were taking place, including an attack in January against a protest march from Belfast to Londonderry that was mounted by off-duty members of the Royal Ulster Constabulary.

On July 12, 1969, the "Glorious Twelfth," the Orange Order marched through Londonderry. As was by now traditionally the case, it provoked an upsell in disorganized violence.[6] This set the tone for the Apprentice Boys parade of August 12, which triggered the infamous battle.

The annual Apprentice Boys parade commemorates the 1689 Siege of Derry, and from the time the tradition began, it has been a source of visceral provocation against Catholics. Agitation began as the parade ran close to the Catholic neighborhood of Bogside, and before long the RUC was fighting pitched battles in the street with Catholic rioters, backed up by Apprentice Boy members and other opportunist Protestants. The situation very quickly slipped out of control, but once the initial mayhem had subsided, it was noticeable that a degree of organization began to creep in. Civil rights leaders began to orchestrate the violence, overwhelming ill-prepared RUC units who responded primarily with teargas and rubber bullets, waiting for reinforcements to arrive. These were rushed in from other metropolitan districts of Northern Ireland.

By August 14, two days after the first attacks, the situation in Bogside had reached a critical

---

[6] The Apprentice Boys is a Protestant fraternal society based then in the city of Londonderry, today called Derry.

point. The entire community was mobilized to one degree or another, and the situation had the appearance of a general insurrection. By then, the RUC had been authorized to distribute firearms, and the B-Specials, a paramilitary police support group, arrived on the scene. Shots were fired and casualties were inflicted.

By afternoon, the Northern Ireland Prime Minister, James Chichester-Clark, was on the telephone with British Prime Minister Harold Wilson to request the deployment of British troops. The British authorities had been on standby for just such a summons, and a company of British soldiers was trucked in from the nearby HMS *Eagle*, a local British shore establishment and naval base.

This was a key moment, representing the first direct military intervention since the partition. Present on the scene was Bernadette Devlin, among a handful of Bogsiders and activists who opposed the deployment of British troops. The RUC, and in particular the B-Specials, were seen quite reasonably as partisan, while British troops, at least for the moment, were identified as neutral.

A picture of Bogside residents during the fighting

Once the violence ended, nobody had been killed, but over 1,000 were injured and the community was in a virtual state of war. Nearly 700 police had been deployed, and they suffered 350 serious injuries. It had been a bloody and sobering episode, named by many as the moment that the "Troubles" began.[7]

---

[7] There is no consensus on precisely when "The Troubles" began, and although the Battle of Bogside is the most often cited, the formation of the

Bloody Sunday

"When it is politically costly for the British to remain in Ireland, they'll go. It won't be triggered until a large number of British soldiers are killed – and that's what's going to happen."
– Danny Morrison

In the wake of the Battle of the Bogside, the welcome afforded to British troops in Northern Ireland did not last very long. The Bogside community renamed the district "Free Derry," a name derived from a mural slogan painted on a gable wall that proclaimed, "You are Now Entering Free Derry." The area then became a self-proclaimed autonomous nationalist area within the city that existed as an RUC no-go zone until 1972. The zone comprised the Bogside and Creggan neighborhoods on the south side of Londonderry, and the authority of the Northern Ireland government was not recognized there.

Louise Price's picture of the mural in 1984

All the while, the unrest continued. On January 30, 1972, a mass demonstration was organized by the Northern Ireland Civil Rights Association (NICRA), attracting about 10,000 people to the Creggan area. The demonstration was ostensibly to protest the internment without trial in August 1971 of 342 individuals suspected to have links with the IRA. This was the result of a controversial program of internment agreed to by the British and Northern Ireland. Men targeted

---

Ulster Volunteer Force is also regarded as an event that triggered The Troubles.

for internment had been gathered up in dawn raids conducted on August 9-10, 1971 and were held in camps adjacent to the notorious Maze Prison. These actions naturally sparked a wave of protests, culminating with a deadly incident on January 30, 1972 now known as Bloody Sunday.

The protest march of January 30 set off from Bishops Field in Creggan at about 2:25 in the afternoon. It began with about 10,000 people, but numbers swelled rapidly as it made its way towards the Guildhall, where a demonstration was to be held outside. En route, however, a system of barricades was encountered, erected by the army to prevent the march from reaching its destination. As the march redirected itself, skirmishes broke out between stone-throwing youth and army details manning the barricades. Soldiers responded by deploying tear gas, rubber bullets, and water cannons.

Nearby, a detachment of the British 1st Battalion, Parachute Regiment was on standby, occupying a derelict three-story building overlooking the route of the march. It was spotted by a group of protesters, and stones began to be thrown at the building. At about 3:55 p.m., the paratroopers opened fire, killing two civilians standing on open ground on the opposite side of the road. In a later inquiry, it was claimed that one man was carrying a black cylindrical object, although both were found later to be unarmed.

Shortly after 4:00 p.m., paratroopers were ordered through the barriers to make as many arrests as they could. On foot, and in armored troop carriers, they chased down rioters, who took refuge in the Bogside. Eyewitnesses claim that people were run down by vehicles, and as troops mingled with rioters, they began seizing people, delivering numerous beatings and firing rubber bullets at close range. A group of about 10 troops took refuge behind a rubble barrier, and as stone-throwing demonstrators approached, they opened fire again, killing six and wounding a seventh.

As the crowd retreated, the troops advanced. Fire was directed at a group occupying a carpark 40-50 yards away, killing two and wounding another four. Moving through the carpark, more shots were fired, and four more were killed. In total, 100 rounds were fired and 13 people lay dead, with many others injured.

The soldiers involved later claimed that they had fired in response to gun and nail bomb attacks by IRA members, and this position was backed up the following day in the House of Commons by the British Home Secretary. At the forefront of condemnation of the episode was Bernadette Devlin, still an independent nationalist MP for Mid Ulster, who accused the British authorities of covering up eyewitness reports that told a very different story.

In Northern Ireland, there was an enormous outcry, and on February 2, the day that 12 of the dead were buried, a general strike almost shut down the Republic of Ireland, the most comprehensive per capita general strike since the end of World War I. Also on February 2, a crowd of 20,000-30,000 protestors gathered at the British embassy in Dublin, where they remained for almost three days. Molotov cocktails were thrown, and the fire brigade was prevented from getting through for several hours as the building burned. Irish Foreign Minister Patrick Hillery petitioned the United Nations for the deployment of a peacekeeping force, and relations between the English and Irish had plunged to their lowest point since the War of Independence over 50 years earlier.

In England, an IRA car bomb exploded outside the barracks of the British Army's 16th Parachute Brigade in Aldershot, claimed later as revenge for Bloody Sunday.

An official tribunal was held, and it issued its findings on April 19. Having taken testimony from numerous sources, the report generally came out in support of the official army version of events. This, however, was not supported by an inquest held into the deaths by the city coroner, who concluded that the army ran amok on what was already informally being called Bloody Sunday. In his report, the coroner, retired British army major Hubert O'Neill, remarked, "These people may have been taking part in a march that was banned but that does not justify the troops coming in and firing live rounds indiscriminately. I would say without hesitation that it was sheer, unadulterated murder. It was murder."

It would not be until 1998 that a non-partisan Royal Commission of Inquiry was authorized by then Prime Minister Tony Blair to try and get to the bottom of what happened on Bloody Sunday. The results of the Inquiry were published on June 15, 2010. Addressing the House of Commons, then Prime Minister David Cameron acknowledged, among other things, that British troops had not only fired the first shot, but had fired on fleeing unarmed civilians, and shot and killed at least one man who was already wounded. A formal apology was then issued by the British government.

After Bloody Sunday, it was feared that Northern Ireland had become ungovernable. Worried about a full-scale war, the British government suspended the Northern Ireland Assembly, returning the territory to direct rule and ending 50 years of uninterrupted Unionist control of the territory.[8] Northern Ireland Prime Minister Brian Faulkner and his cabinet resigned immediately in protest, and while they met for the last time, Stormont, the seat of Northern Irish authority, was besieged by some 100,000 unionists staging a protest strike that brought the city of Belfast to a standstill. Power now resided in the hands of the new Secretary of State for Northern Ireland, and the Northern Ireland Office retained responsibility for the day-to-day running of the province. Although a power-sharing assembly was attempted in 1973, direct rule was, for the time being at least, back to stay.

The Violence Continues

"I want to make it perfectly clear that terrorism and extremism in the community cannot be tolerated, that the rule of law and justice must be restored." – William Whitelaw, Secretary of

---

[8] This was contained the Northern Ireland (Temporary Provisions) Act 1972, effective 30 March 1972.

State for Northern Ireland

Bloody Sunday and its aftermath created a situation of general hostility in Northern Ireland towards the British government and British troops, adding to the multiple issues already scarring the social and political landscape. The IRA had split early in 1969 into the Official and Provisional IRA, the latter with a more active agenda. The Provisional IRA, or the "Provos," was a radical Catholic nationalist paramilitary organization most active on the front line, while the Official IRA tended to be more political, ideologically aligned and less active. The Provisional IRA began to gather improved support after Bloody Sunday, raising fresh drafts of recruits and increasing operations.

The Provisional IRA, known by the authorities simply as the IRA, began its campaign early in 1971, and by the end of the following year, over 100 members of the security forces had been killed in operations, and 500 others were injured. In all, about 1,300 bombings had been carried out, making the group's violent aims clear.

The Provos sourced most of their funding from the United States, channeled through an organization known as NORAID, or the Irish Northern Aid Committee. Established in 1920, NORAID became the main vehicle of IRA funding, and it would remain active until the end of the Troubles. It continues to exist today.[9]

A fundraising letter sent out in 1971 and 1972 told readers, "Our support goes exclusively to the Provisional IRA and those who are working with them. Where does the money go? Our funds are channelled through Joe Cahill of Belfast to be used for the advancement of the campaign in Northern Ireland. What is the relationship between the IRA and Noraid? We are fighting a guerrilla war and will continue to do so. We, the members of the Provisional Irish Republican Army, will fight and die until victory is ours. Remember, the Irish Northern Aid Committee is the only organization in America that supports the Provisional IRA."[10]

All the while, the attacks continued. A bombing campaign killed numerous civilians, peaking on July 22, 1972 when 22 bombs were detonated in the center of Belfast. Seven civilians and two British soldiers were killed in a day known as Bloody Friday. British troop concentrations peaked at 20 per 1,000 among the civilian population, the largest British military operation since the War of Independence. In total, about 20,000 British troops were active in Northern Ireland.

The political process, as all of this was taking place, saw exploratory talks between the British government and the Provisional IRA. These talks were held in secret between the Secretary of State for Northern Ireland, William Whitelaw, and six IRA leaders. The two sides met on July 7, 1972, during a two-week ceasefire. Whitelaw suffered no small amount of criticism for this in

---

[9] During the 1980s, Colonel Muammar Gaddafi contributed arms and funding to the IRA.

[10] Washington Post, 22 March 1987.

the House of Commons, but it displayed considerable delicacy and diplomatic skill on his part that he was able to arrange a face-to-face meeting at all. Discussions took place in a private house in London and lasted three hours, but the IRA simply restated what were by then regarded as routine and unworkable demands. These required a total withdrawal of British forces, the right to self-determination by the Irish people, and an amnesty for those the group considered political prisoners. Naturally, the British government was unlikely to concede to anything like this, but before Whitelaw had an opportunity to put the matter before Parliament, the ceasefire collapsed and the violence in Belfast resumed.

The next milestone in what might be regarded as a peace process was an attempt to establish a power-sharing executive in Northern Ireland and a Council of Ireland as a preliminary all-Ireland legislative body, operating with limited jurisdiction. This was known as the Sunningdale Agreement. The accord was signed on December 9, 1973 in the Berkshire village of Sunningdale. According to the *BBC*, "Tripartite talks on Northern Ireland [have] ended in an historic agreement to set up a Council of Ireland."

The accord marked in some respects the conclusion of Whitelaw's efforts to broker an acceptable peace in Northern Ireland, and it is debatable, behind the official hubris, if it ever had any chance of succeeding. Unionists were split, and the IRA was in absolute opposition, with its objective remaining a complete and undiluted reunification of Ireland.

The official Unionist position on any power-sharing solution was that it was simply impractical. To them, no cooperation was possible with an entity sworn to its destruction. There were also deep suspicions that the Council of Ireland was simply an all-Ireland Parliament in waiting. In the end, the accord was sunk by ongoing violence before it even got off the ground. A general strike was organized, and it was dealt with rather lethargically by the authorities, causing nationalists to argue that the British had done nothing to support its own initiative.

In and of itself, the Sunningdale Agreement was of little value for the peace process, but it offered insight into how intractable the political situation was. The gap between the stated objectives of the main paramilitary organizations was simply too vast for there to be any hope of a political solution to bridge it. The exertion taken to negotiate the agreements reads somewhat like a formularized effort to simply keep the matter alive, with no real expectation of success. Some historians claim that the British foreign intelligence organization, MI5, played a hand in the organization of demonstrations and protests in Northern Ireland, reacting against the foreign policy of the unpopular Prime Minister Harold Wilson.

The pro-Sunningdale Unionists, briefly sworn in, resigned, and that, for all intents and purposes, was that. The new power-sharing regime collapsed, and on May 17, 1974, three car bombs were detonated without warning in Dublin's city center. Responsibility for these was claimed by the Ulster Volunteer Force. 26 people died and nearly 300 were injured. 90 minutes later, in Monaghan, close to the Northern Ireland border, a fourth bomb exploded, killing seven more people. Peace was certainly not the first choice of the paramilitaries.

In November 1974, a bill was introduced into the British House of Commons which would quickly emerge as the "Prevention of Terrorism Act of 1974." This act was not only tabled in response to acts of terrorism occurring on an almost daily basis, but in particular because of a series of pub bombings that rocked Birmingham during that month, claiming the lives of 21 and injuring 184 more. The Act came into effect on the mainland immediately, and soon afterwards in Northern Ireland.

The Prevention of Terrorism Act was robust and extremely wide-ranging, with provisions to limit and proscribe organizations, enact exclusion orders, target terror financing, and various standards of arrest and detention. The Republic of Ireland implemented a similar state of emergency after the assassination of the British ambassador to the Republic of Ireland, Christopher Ewart-Biggs, on July 21, 1976. A landmine had been placed outside his official residence in Sandyford, Co. Dublin.

Hunger Strikes and Political Prisoners

"They have nothing in their whole imperial arsenal that can break the spirit of one Irishman who doesn't want to be broken." – Bobby Sands

The year 1979 was eventful. On March 31, a bomb exploded in a car as it exited the House of Commons car park, instantly killing its driver, Airey Neave, the member for Abington and Conservative shadow secretary for Northern Ireland.[11] The killing was perpetrated by members of the Irish National Liberation Army (INLA), the paramilitary wing of the Irish Republican Socialist Party and yet another violent participant in the Troubles.

A few months earlier, on February 20, 11 men of a murderous loyalist gang known as the Shankill Butchers were convicted of a total of 19 murders, bringing them a total of 42 life sentences. The Shankill Butchers have tended in recent years to be regarded less as a political enforcement gang than sociopathic murderers operating under a vague loyalist agenda. Catholics were often kidnapped at random, brutally tortured, and killed, usually with their throats cut. Several loyalists also suffered the same fate as a result of personal disputes. Whatever the motivation, these killings introduced a new and disturbing scale to the violence in Northern Ireland. Concluding sentencing, the judge overseeing the trial remarked that these crimes represented "a lasting monument to blind sectarian bigotry."

By 1979, the spillover of Northern Irish violence was regularly being felt on the English mainland, and periodically in Scotland. A few days before the conclusion of the Shankill Butchers trial, two pubs frequented by Catholics in Glasgow were bombed. But the most

---

[11] Airey Neve was Conservative Margaret Thatcher's choice of Northern Ireland Secretary, and he promised hard-line measures in respect of Thatcher's own tough position. Margaret Thatcher was generally expected to be the next prime minister.

notorious incident as far as the British were concerned was the August 1979 assassination of Lord Mountbatten, a seminal figure in 20th century British history and a member of the extended royal family.

Mountbatten

As usual, the Mountbatten family spent the summer at Classiebawn Castle, located on the coast of County Sligo, in the Republic of Ireland just a few miles from the Northern Ireland border. On August 27, Mountbatten and several family members set off lobster-potting on a small boat that had been rigged the night before with a 50 pound bomb by an IRA operative. A few hundred yards offshore, the bomb was remotely detonated. The bomb destroyed the boat killing Mountbatten and two of his grandchildren, along with injuring a few others. On the same day Mountbatten was killed, 18 British soldiers, among them 16 from the Parachute Regiment, were killed in an IRA ambush staged just south of Newry.

The violence shocked the British public, and the IRA quickly claimed responsibility. However, more horrifying yet was a statement delivered six weeks later by Sinn Féin vice-president Gerry Adams, who openly condoned the killings as a legitimate act of war. He claimed, "What the IRA did to him is what Mountbatten had been doing all his life to other people; and with his war record I don't think he could have objected to dying in what was clearly a war situation."[12] If

Gerry Adams was already persona non grata in the United Kingdom, he was now regarded with utter and undisguised revulsion.

Adams

Throughout this time, prisons represented yet another front in the ongoing conflict, especially Maze Prison, where IRA members and others convicted of terrorism offences were held. A perennial issue was always the status of individuals convicted under prevention of terrorism statutes, who were typically classified as criminals, but who demanded the classification of prisoners of war.

The first hunger strike over this issue was staged by IRA members in Crumlin Road Gaol in Belfast. This occurred during the talks held between Whitelaw and members of the Provisional IRA, and Whitelaw was anxious not to rock the boat. He conferred a "Special Category" status for those convicted of terrorism-related offences, but four years later, under different circumstances and a different administration, this status was withdrawn. After March 1976, anyone convicted of a terrorism-related crime would be housed in the newly completed "H"

---

[12] Sinn Féin, meaning in the Irish "We Ourselves," or "Ourselves Alone."

Block section of Maze Prison in Northern Ireland. That prison is located about 14 miles south of Belfast, and it had been the site of long-term internments from as early as 1971. By 1976, the distinctive "H" Blocks had themselves become a center and symbol of protest against the Special Category status.

Patrick McAleer's picture of one of the corridors in H4

Wilson Adams' picture of the prison

Protests took on many forms. One was the "Blanketmen" protest, an action by IRA members who refused to wear prison clothing and thus covered themselves with blankets. A "No Wash" or "Dirty" protest began in 1978, protesting the sanitary conditions.

This, in many respects, was the publicity branch of the IRA. Ongoing resistance within the prison system was eye-catching, and the hunger strikes in particular captured public attention. On October 27, 1980, seven prisoners at the Maze Prison launched a determined hunger strike. Their demands on the surface were not unreasonable, consisting only of the right to wear what clothes they chose, exemption from prison work, freedom of association and the right to organize their own leisure activities. These, however, were terms of POW status, and the government would not yield.

In power at No. 10 Downing Street was Conservative Prime Minister Margaret Thatcher, and she was certainly in no mood to trifle with the IRA. She was determined to destroy the organization, and no expressions of sympathy or concern found their way from Westminster to the Maze. The IRA were bombing targets across England, including the Chelsea Barracks, which killed two British soldiers, and as a result, the British weren't exactly going to be lenient.

That hunger strike soon faltered, but it was renewed in the spring of 1981, and this time it was led by Member of Parliament for Fermanagh and South Tyrone, the Right Honourable Bobby

Sands.[13] Bobby Sands also happened to be a member of the Provisional IRA who was convicted of firearms offences, and he was serving a 14-year sentence. He was behind numerous protests, and on March 1, he began refusing food. This hunger strike was deliberately staggered to maintain steady pressure on the British government, which did not yield an inch. On May 5, 66 days into his hunger strike, Sands died. Within two weeks of his funeral, three more hunger strikers were dead.[14]

In June, the Catholic Commission for Justice and Peace stepped in and presented the British government with a number of proposals. The impasse was broken, and before long, all but freedom of association was granted. It was a heavy price to pay, and a rather nominal reward, but the propaganda value of the action was immeasurable. It was also a powerful symbolic point of reference for the Republicans and Northern Irish Catholics, and it energized the IRA and brought Sinn Féin back into relevance. The mantra of the Republican movement was now "The Armalite and the Ballot Box."

Margaret Thatcher had entered office in May 1979 with plenty of Northern Irish issues high on the agenda. The killings of Airey Neve and Lord Mountbatten demanded an answer, and her policy for the time being was simply to establish a security force victory over the paramilitaries. She intended to negotiate, but only at her leisure, and only from a position of strength.

---

[13] Bobby Sands was nominated to the seat after the death of the incumbent. Sands was already four days into the hunger strike.

[14] In total, ten hunger strikers died in the 217 days of the hunger strike, seven from the Provisional IRA and three from the Irish National Liberation Army.

Thatcher

Her attitude to the hunger strike was no less resolute. She was girding to deal with a British miners' strike, and in every corner, her answer was precisely the same: tough, direct and determined action. The hunger strikers could accept the consequences of their actions, and many did.

In July 1982, two particularly heinous bombings occurred in Hyde Park and Regent's Park in London. Both targeted military processions and killed 18 military personnel in total, including seven bandmembers performing on a gazebo. The attack was brazen and bloody, with numerous civilian injuries and the deaths and dismemberment of several horses. Images of the gory aftermath saturated news reportage in the days that followed.

Thatcher's relationship with the Republic of Ireland was also frosty at best, and the tone of relations plummeted even further during the Falklands War. During the Argentine invasion of the Falklands, Thatcher took an uncompromising position, and with very little preamble dispatched a naval task force to settle the matter. Ireland did not support this action in the United Nations

Security Council, however, as she had assumed it would, but instead called, through the United Nations, for an immediate ceasefire upon the sinking of the *General Belgrano*. Thatcher did not easily forgive that.

Thatcher herself then became the IRA's primary target, and as the tempo of hostilities between the two sides continued to be high, the IRA pulled off one of its most audacious operations. In the early hours of October 12, 1984, a bomb ripped through several floors of the Grand Hotel in Brighton, which were housing delegates to the Conservative Party annual conference. Thatcher narrowly avoided injury - the bomb destroyed most of her bathroom, but the living and sleeping areas of her suite were undamaged. Five people were killed, however, including Trade Secretary Norman Tebbit.

The following day, the IRA issued a statement claiming responsibility, adding that it would try again. The statement began with a chilling warning: "Mrs. Thatcher will now realize that Britain cannot occupy our country and torture our prisoners and shoot our people in their own streets and get away with it."

That may have been true, but what was also true is that the IRA could not expect to get away with attacking Britain's prime minister. She addressed the conference at 09:30 the following morning, delivering a composed and compact address confirming Britain's resolve and vowing that those responsible would pay. This won her universal admiration, and very little public sympathy went to the IRA, or any part of Ireland for that matter.

Despite this, and despite a continuation of the tough talk, a little over a year later, Thatcher put her signature to the Anglo-Irish Agreement of 1985, a move that surprised many observers. There was, however, pressure being brought to bear against her from many quarters. These included the direct effects of the conflict itself – IRA bombings had a powerful psychological effect – and also from various political sources, the most important of which was the United States. Anglo-Irish talks had for some time already been underway, but more as background noise than any serious effort. Under pressure from Ronald Reagan, whom Thatcher held in very high regard, things began to slip into gear.

In general terms, the agreement gave the Republic of Ireland an advisory role in the government of Northern Ireland, by way of a framework for intergovernmental consultation. It was an advance across a very limited front, but it was enough to provoke resignations from Thatcher's cabinet and a furious rejection of any aspect of it by the Ulster Unionists. Even still, it was a thin legislative thread linking the two territories, and could only be seen as a signal for a more concerted push. Thatcher was accused of treachery by Unionist MPs, but in general, the accord received wide bipartisan support. The agreement was signed on November 15, 1985, at Hillsborough Castle, Northern Ireland, by Thatcher and the Irish Taoiseach, Garret FitzGerald.

Thatcher may have been negotiating, but she did not ease the pressure being put on the paramilitaries, and her security regime in Northern Ireland was as tough as ever. She discussed with the permanent secretary the reintroduction of internment, and when she was dissuaded from that, she introduced the iconic broadcast ban. On October 19, 1988, a notice was issued by the Home Secretary prohibiting the broadcast of direct statements by representatives or supporters of 11 Irish political and military organizations. The ban prohibited the UK news media from any broadcast of the voices (though not the words) of 10 prominent Irish republican and Ulster loyalist paramilitary groups, as well as Sinn Féin.

Other groups were also affected, but the ban was directed mainly at Sinn Féin, and particularly its leader Gerry Adams, a figure of deep revulsion among loyalists and the British general public. This, however, resulted in the absurd situation of actors reading statements made by Gerry Adams, offering him a degree of recognition that he certainly did not enjoy before.

In the meantime, another bloody year passed. In March 1988, the British people were shocked once again by an incident now known as the Corporal Killings. Two British army personnel accidentally drove into an IRA funeral procession, and when they were identified and targeted, they were dragged out of their car and beaten and shot. Their bodies were left bloodied and naked in the open. The event was captured by an overhead news camera, and the following day, graphic images flooded British living rooms.

The Peace Process

"In the past I have defended the right of the IRA to engage in armed struggle. I did so because there was no alternative for those who would not bend the knee, or turn a blind eye to oppression, or for those who wanted a national republic." - Gerry Adams

The Remembrance Day Bombing, a notorious IRA attack against a commemoration in the Northern Ireland town of Enniskillen, was the first action to be acknowledged by the IRA as a mistake. 11 people were killed and scores injured on November 8, 1987 when a device was detonated at the town's war memorial, where a large crowd had gathered. The injured were on the whole elderly people, and the mistake, as the IRA was prepared to admit it, was simply because it intended the bomb to target a parade of troops. Gerry Adams, however, admitted that an act of that nature undermined the legitimate use of force in the armed struggle.

Historians have often pointed to that moment as marking a shift in the Republican mindset. The war in Northern Ireland had reached a virtual stalemate, and British security coverage in Northern Ireland was deeply impacting the ability of the IRA to wage war.

Adams was by then the public face of Irish nationalism, although, as leader of Sinn Féin, he was careful to distance himself from the paramilitary activities of the IRA. For his part, he was a charismatic and fearless politician who allowed enough militant and anti-British rhetoric to escape his lips, and he tacitly promoted IRA atrocities by his refusal to condemn them. As a result, he became the focus of British opposition to the IRA, and the man the British most loved to hate. By the late 1980s, however, Adams' words were more carefully chosen, and his rhetoric was noticeably softer.

Another rising star in the Irish nationalist movement was Martin McGuinness, a self-proclaimed IRA member now reinventing himself as a nationalist politician and Sinn Féin member. Unlike Adams, Martin McGuinness made little secret of his engagement in IRA violence, and his image in IRA fatigues, ranked at various funerals and other public events, depicted him as a sort of gangster. These were men who appeared to the British public to be little more than sociopathic killers, which, in fact, more than a few were.

McGuinness

For there to be any movement beyond this mutual loathing, there seemed to be a need to display the kind of political gymnastics simply impossible to imagine on either side. On the Unionist side, there were personalities no less polarizing and provocative, such as Ian Paisley. Paisley was a tall and heavy-set man, and with a pronounced Ulster brogue, his voice was frequently heard on nightly newscasts promoting an uncompromising Unionist position. It was he who both implicitly and explicitly allowed it to be known that war was an acceptable option in order to retain Northern Irish links with Britain.

In the end, it was a 51-year-old opposition leader in the Northern Ireland assembly who opened the lines of communication. Leader of the Social Democratic and Labour Party, John Hume, was sufficiently unthreatening to raise no hackles. He was at the time a quiet, avuncular man who nonetheless wielded great political skill. He approached the issue indirectly, dealing first with Irish nationalists based in the United States. At the same time, the Reagan-Thatcher relationship was such that influence existed to be brought to bear against the British establishment itself. President Reagan seldom missed an opportunity to highlight his Irish roots.

Thatcher would later grumble that the American president forced her to do it, but what is also inescapable is that the time was simply right. The populations of both territories were ready, and it had become by then manifestly clear that outright victory for either side was impossible. As Hume himself put it, "Ireland is not a romantic dream; it is not a flag; it is 4.5 million people divided into two powerful traditions. The solution will be found not on the basis of victory for either, but on the basis of agreement and a partnership between both. The real division of Ireland is not a line drawn on the map but in the minds and hearts of its people."

Preliminary discussions between John Hume and Gerry Adams began sometime in early 1988, and though they were secret discussions initially, word soon leaked. Once the initial discomfiture of both sides had adjusted to that fact, a steady rate of progress was made. The talks took place against a backdrop of ongoing IRA violence and the implementation of the British broadcasting ban, so there was a certain amount of inevitable cynicism from all sides.

Hume at that moment was perhaps negotiating from a position of strength, and his basic principle was the right of self-determination for both communities in Ireland. This required Adams to step over a threshold he had to date never been willing to consider, let alone cross. It was an outcome somewhat less than a full and united republic – the stated Republican goal - which would acknowledge the right of Northern Irish unionists to hold an opposing position. It also required the IRA to lay down its weapons. Nonetheless, the uncompromising façade that Adams had maintained throughout his public career to date began to crack, and in March 1989, he issued a simple public statement that said he desired a non-armed political movement to work towards self-determination.

This certainly was a shift in a very different direction for Adams, and whatever had been going on behind closed doors, it seemed to be working. This statement was followed by an admission made by the Northern Ireland Secretary Peter Brook that the point had been reached that the IRA could not be defeated militarily, adding a little more honesty to the murky mix. He added shortly afterwards that unification was not off the table as far as the British were concerned, and if, in the spirit of self-determination, it proved to be the popular option, then the British had neither selfish nor strategic interests in stopping it.

The question, however, remained one of self-determination, and the likelihood of a clean-cut solution along those lines was as remote as it had been a century earlier. A more creative solution than this was required, but openly expressed sentiments further smoothed the path towards more formal contacts, and perhaps even an agreement.

In 1990, major international changes were underway in the wake of the Berlin Wall's demise and the crumbling Soviet Union. Dictatorships and despised regimes around the world began to collapse as old patronages passed away, and corrosive regional insurgencies in many regions of the world suddenly found their relevance waning, but more importantly, their funding was diminishing.

In the spring of 1991, the first formal round-table discussions began. Sinn Féin was excluded simply because that would be a bridge too far at such an early stage of negotiations, and there was no British or Unionist politician prepared to share a room, let alone a table, with any member of such a despised organization. But that was to be expected, and Gerry Adams did not throw up any obstacles. Instead, an increase of violence on all sides reminded everyone involved that the war was still very much ongoing.

Talks were held between British and Northern Ireland delegates, and in general the process was aimed at reaching unanimity among discordant Unionists who were divided among themselves. In May 1992, Northern Ireland Secretary Peter Brook held a lengthy meeting with Unionist leaders in London. James Molyneaux, then leader of the Ulster Unionist Party (UUP), and Ian Paisley, then leader of the Democratic Unionist Party (DUP), announced afterwards that they were "well satisfied with the results."

Similar contacts continued, and on July 1, Ulster Unionists agreed for the first time to hold talks with the Irish government. In April the following year, the open secret of the talks was made public with a joint statement confirming their mutual commitment to self-determination. The statement noted, "We are mindful that not all the people of Ireland share that view or agree on how to give meaningful expression to it." Later, in private, Hume expressed his optimism that not only London was shifting towards a neutral position, but that the Republicans could be convinced to reject violence. That still seemed like a long shot, no doubt, but Adams was a powerful Republican voice, and if his position could be moderated, then anyone's could.

Violence and bombing continued, and on October 23, 1993, an IRA bomb exploded on the Shankill Road in Belfast, killing 10 people and injuring numerous others. This prompted a wave of reprisals as loyalist paramilitaries sought revenge for the killings.

By then, Thatcher had left No. 10 Downing Street and a more moderate figure in the form of Prime Minister John Major had taken up occupancy. By the end of 1993, Major was prepared to admit that secret communications between the IRA and the British government had been underway between MI5 and the IRA, and that the result of these was an acknowledgement by the IRA that violence had run its course and that the organization now needed assistance to bring the conflict to a close. If true, this certainly was a shift, and while loyalists continued their direct action, killing six Catholic men in a bar in County Down, the IRA issued a statement in August 1994 declaring a ceasefire. The statement said, "Recognizing the potential of the current situation and in order to enhance the democratic process and underlying our definitive commitment to its success, the leadership of the IRA have decided that as of midnight, August 31, there will be a complete cessation of military operations. All our units have been instructed accordingly. We believe that an opportunity to secure a just and lasting settlement has been created."

Major

Things then slipped into a higher gear. President Bill Clinton sanctioned a visa for Gerry Adams to visit the United States, and a joint declaration by the British and Irish prime ministers, the Downing Street Declaration in December 1993, confirmed the common commitment of the two governments to self-determination.

This, then, became the basis of the discussions. The broadcasting ban against Sinn Féin was lifted, and the combined loyalist military command announced a reciprocating ceasefire. The accompanying statement, issued on October 13, 1994, read, "We are on the threshold of a new and exciting beginning with our battles in future being political battles, fought on the side of honesty, decency and democracy against the negativity of mistrust, misunderstanding and malevolence, so that, together, we can bring forth a wholesome society in which our children, and their children, will know the meaning of true peace."

Preliminary announcements of disarmament preceded the first official meeting in 23 years between Sinn Féin and British government officials, held in the spring of 1995. Later that year, President Clinton made his first official visit to Ireland, revealing a diplomatic influence that analysts have since acknowledged was pivotal to the forward momentum of the process.

The violence was not over, and the IRA broke the ceasefire with a major bombing that targeted London's Canary Warf, alienating itself and Sinn Féin once again. The Mitchell Report, however, released in February 1996, acknowledged that the IRA could not be reasonably expected to disarm before formal talks, and that position was broadly accepted.[15] In June of that year, the IRA bombed Manchester, destroying a large part of the city center. Early the following year, Lance Bombardier Stephen Restorick was killed in Northern Ireland, an unremarkable event other than that his would be the last killing of a British soldier in Northern Ireland.

Two months later, Labour Prime Minister Tony Blair walked across the threshold of No. 10 Downing Street, and a strong bond was formed with Clinton. A significant amount of diplomatic skill was then brought to bear, which was essential in bringing the still bickering stakeholders to a formal session of peace talks. Northern Ireland Secretary Mo Mowlam, against a backdrop of fierce criticism, visited loyalist inmates in the Maze Prison to urge them to support the pending peace talks. Prime Minister Blair announced a formal commission of inquiry into the Bloody Sunday massacre, and in general a concerted effort to heal the division was palpable.

By the spring of 1998, all of Northern Ireland signed up for what was known already as the Good Friday Agreement. At 5.30 p.m. on Friday, April 10, 1998, U.S. Senator George Mitchell stated, "I am pleased to announce that the two governments and the political parties in Northern Ireland have reached agreement." The agreement was signed in Belfast by British and Irish Prime Ministers Tony Blair and Bertie Ahern.

The IRA refused to endorse the agreement, however, and it would not commit to decommissioning. Elements within the armed wing opposed to Sinn Féin's political involvement broke away to form the "Real IRA," but this seemed a rather forlorn and desperate last resort. A referendum in Northern Ireland returned a result of 71% in favor of a settlement.

The agreement, also known as the Belfast Agreement, included proposals for a Northern Ireland Assembly with a power-sharing executive, new cross-border institutions with the Republic of Ireland, and a body linking devolved assemblies across the United Kingdom with Westminster and Dublin. In addition, the Republic of Ireland agreed to drop its constitutional claim to the six counties which formed Northern Ireland. There were also proposals on the decommissioning of paramilitary weapons, the future of policing in Northern Ireland, and the early release of paramilitary prisoners.

---

[15] The Mitchel Commission was conducted by US Senator George J. Mitchell.

In August 1998, the IRA bombed the city center of Omagh, killing 29 people and two unborn babies. In response to this, the most murderous attack of the conflict, Gerry Adams said, "The violence we have seen must be for all of us now a thing of the past, over, done with and gone."

By the end of 1998, security installation demolitions had begun and the first phased release of political prisoners began. Arms decommissioning would prove more problematic, and a significant amount of minor bickering was still heard as sworn enemies of the past attempted to adjust to a new reality. In November 1999, however, practical power-sharing began.

In practical terms, the Good Friday Agreement came into effect in December 1998 as Northern Ireland politicians took their seats at the Irish assembly in Stormont, but a turbulent period still lay ahead as all of the old irritations, such as the annual Orange marches, continued to keep bruised sensibilities painful. Given the past, decommissioning was never likely to be easy. Dissident paramilitaries maintained their activities in an effort to derail the agreement, the worst instance of which was the Omagh bombing cited above.

The combined assembly limped on through three suspensions before a fourth suspension saw a reimposition in October 2002 of direct rule in Northern Ireland. Devolution resumed only in 2007, following the amendments known as the St Andrew's Agreement of 2006. When the assembly returned to business in March 2007, the loyalist DUP's Ian Paisley became First Minister and Republican Sinn Féin's Martin McGuinness became the Deputy First Minister.

The fact that two such polar opposites, a decade earlier at one another's throats, could cooperate on the floor of the same assembly served as a symbol of just how far Northern Ireland had come from the darkest days of the Troubles.

Online Resources

Other Irish history titles by Charles River Editors

Other titles about Ireland on Amazon

Bibliography

Arnold, Bruce (1977). Irish Art: A Concise History. London: Thames & Hudson. p. 180. ISBN 0-500-20148-X.

Becker, Annette; Wang, Wilfried (1997). 20th-century Architecture: Ireland. Munich: Prestel. p. 198. ISBN 3-7913-1719-9.

Collins, Neil; Cradden, Terry (2001). Irish Politics Today. Manchester University Press. p. 163. ISBN 0-7190-6174-1.

Cullinane, J.P. (1973). Phycology of the south coast of Ireland. University College

Cork.

Dennison, Gabriel; Ni Fhloinn, Baibre (1994). Traditional Architecture in Ireland. Dublin: Environmental Institute, University College Dublin. p. 94. ISBN 1-898473-09-9.

Dooney, Sean; O'Toole, John (1992). Irish Government Today. Dublin: Gill and Macmillan. p. 247. ISBN 0-7171-1703-0.

Ellis, Steven G. (1921). The Story of the Irish Race: A Popular History of Ireland. Ireland: The Irish Publishing Co. p. 768. ISBN 0-517-06408-1.

Fairley, J.S. (1975). An Irish Beast Book. A Natural History of Ireland's Furred Wildlife. Blackstaff Press, Belfast. ISBN 0-85640-090-4.

Foster, Robert Fitzroy (1988). Modern Ireland, 1600–1972. Penguin Books. p. 688. ISBN 0-7139-9010-4.

Hackney, P. Ed. (1992). Stewart and Corry's Flora of the North-east of Ireland. Belfast: Institute of Irish Studies, The Queen's University. ISBN 0-85389-446-9.

Haigh, A.; Lawton, C. (2007). "Wild mammals of an Irish urban forest". The Irish Naturalists' Journal. Belfast: I.N.J. Committee. 28 (10): 395–403. ISSN 0021-1311.

Hardy, F. G.; Guiry, M. D. (2006). A Check-list and Atlas of the Seaweeds of Britain and Ireland (revised ed.). London: British Phycological Society. pp. x, 435. ISBN 3-906166-35-X.

Herm, Gerhard (2002). The Celts. Ireland: St. Martin's Press. ISBN 0-312-31343-8.

Knowles, M.C. (1929). "The Lichens of Ireland". Proceedings of the Royal Irish Academy. 38: 179–434.

Morton, O. (1994). Marine Algae of Northern Ireland. Ulster Museum. ISBN 0-900761-28-8.

Morton, O. (2003). "The marine algae macroalgae of County Donegal, Ireland". Bulletin Irish biogeog. Society. 27: 3–164.

Nunn, J.D. (2002). Marine Biodiversity in Ireland and Adjacent Waters. Proceedings of a Conference 26–27 April 2001. Belfast: Ulster Museum.

O'Croinin, Daibhi (2005). Prehistoric and Early Ireland. Oxford University Press. p. 1219. ISBN 0-19-821737-4.

Ó Gráda, Cormac (1997). A Rocky Road: The Irish Economy Since the 1920s. Manchester University Press. p. 246. ISBN 0-7190-4584-3.

Oppenheimer, Stephen (2006). Origins of the British: A Genetic Detective Story. New York: Carroll & Graf. p. 534. ISBN 0-7867-1890-0.

O'Rahilly, T. F. (1947). Early Irish History and Mythology. Medieval Academy of America.

Scannell, Mary J. P.; Synnott, Donal M. (1972). Census catalogue of the flora of Ireland. Dublin: Department of Agriculture & Fisheries.

Seaward, M. R. D. (1984). "Census Catalogue of Irish Lichens". Glasra. 8: 1–32.

Woodcock, N. H.; Strachan, Robin A. (2000). Geological History of Britain and Ireland. Hoboken: Blackwell Publishing. p. 423. ISBN 0-632-03656-7.

Wallis, Geoff; Wilson, Sue (2001). The Rough Guide to Irish Music. Rough Guides. p. 599. ISBN 1-85828-642-5.

Free Books by Charles River Editors

We have brand new titles available for free most days of the week. To see which of our titles are currently free, click on this link.

Discounted Books by Charles River Editors

We have titles at a discount price of just 99 cents everyday. To see which of our titles are currently 99 cents, click on this link.

Printed in Great Britain
by Amazon